THE OTHER ALCATRAZ

Home of the Western Gull

By
Ernest B. Lageson &
Jeanne Lettiere Lageson

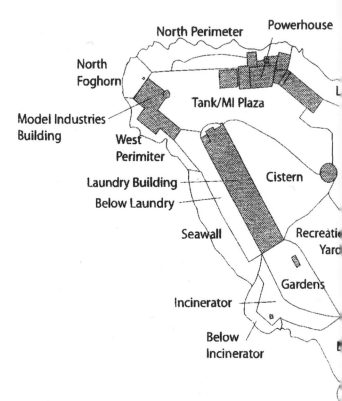

Western Gull census areas on Alcatraz

ways

Post Exchange/Officer's Club

Upper Walkways

Roofs

Dock

Cellhouse

h

Lighthouse

Eucalyptus

Parade Ground

Rubble Piles

Agave Trail

Photographs by Ernest and Jeanne Lageson
Sketches by Jeanne Lageson
Cover design by Ernie Lageson

Library of Congress Control Number 2006909899
ISBN 1424323142

LAGESON PRESS

Kensington, California

Dedication

To Stan Zbikowski, a dedicated friend of
all the birds on Alcatraz

Acknowledgments

We wish to express our thanks to the Alcatraz National Park Service personnel for their assistance in making this book a reality. In particular, Biologist Christian Hellwig was extremely helpful. Christian not only provided encouragement and support, but made many of his technical and professional publications available for research and background. He also reviewed the manuscript for technical accuracy and made himself available to answer all our questions.

The Alcatraz Rangers gave us full access to the island during several nesting seasons to permit us to do the extensive photography required to complete the book. In this regard we received considerable assistance from Ian Miyashiro, a Wildlife Intern, who guided us through the Western Gull neighborhoods, and to various nesting sites. Ranger Lori Brosnan assisted by reviewing the manuscript and offering her suggestions.

A special word is appropriate regarding Stanley Zbikowski to whom this book is dedicated. Stan served for more than twenty years as Sales Manager of the Alcatraz retail stores, a job he held from its inception until his untimely death in 2005 He is missed greatly by all who knew him. A dedicated supporter of all the bird life on Alcatraz, Stan provided boundless support and encouragement for the book. His energy and support for the project have been carried on by his successor, Chris Warren, and Lala Macabagal of the Alcatraz staff.

Don Ellis of Authorconnect.com, and Wayne Pope of Pope Graphic Arts Center, friends and colleagues both, provided invaluable editorial and technical assistance during the publication of the book.

Finally, we were aided substantially by our own immediate family. Our son, Ernie Lageson III, designed the cover of the book and assisted in the artistic details. Our grandchildren, Beau and Anna Cardall, and Jacqueline, Caroline, and Ben Lageson all read and critiqued the manuscript from the young reader's perspective. Beau also assisted his uncle in the design of the cover. It was truly a family project.

THE
OTHER ALCATRAZ

A Brief History

For centuries, Alcatraz has been the scene of family life. During a few of its thousands of years of existence, human families occupied the island, but for most of the time, bird families have been its major inhabitants. History suggests that when Alcatraz was first discovered by Europeans, the dominant bird there was the pelican, but pelicans have not lived on the island for well over a hundred years. The major resident in recent years has been the Western Gull. This is the story of the Western Gull and its life on Alcatraz today.

There is fossil evidence that the Western Gull has lived on the Pacific Coast for tens of thousands of years. Throughout these years Alcatraz has been home to a variety of birds including, not only gulls, but pelicans, herons, egrets, hawks, ravens, cormorants and many others. Since there were virtually no natural enemies of the birds living on the island, their population flourished. The Native Americans of the San Francisco Bay

Area, the Ohlone and Miwok tribes, did not live on the island, but occasionally visited Alcatraz to fish from its rocky shores and collect eggs from the many birds' nests located there.

Although European explorers sailed near San Francisco Bay as early as 1542, the bay and its many islands were not discovered by outsiders until 1769. Juan Cabrillo, a Spanish explorer, sailed north along the California coast in 1542, but did not see the Golden Gate. In 1579 the English explorer Sir Francis Drake sailed along the coast and discovered what today is Drake's Bay, but he too missed San Francisco Bay. In 1602 Sebastian Vizcaino sailed north from a Spanish settlement in Mexico searching for northern ports in order to increase trade with the Far East. During his voyage he discovered Monterey Bay, approximately one hundred miles south of San Francisco.

When the government of Spain learned that the Russians had occupied parts of Alaska and were preparing to sail south, they considered this to be a threat to their control of the California Territory, much of which was then unexplored. In an effort to explore and map the area, an expedition was sent north from the Spanish settlement in San Diego. The party was under the command of Gaspar de Portola, the military governor of Upper California. Among his group was Father Junipero Serra, the Franciscan Catholic priest who developed the extensive mission system throughout Central and Southern California. In search of a land route to Monterey Bay, the expedition missed its intended destination, but on October 31, 1769 after a five-month march became the first non-natives to look upon San Francisco Bay.

It was not until 1775, however, that detailed exploration and mapping of the bay was done. On August 5th of that year Don Juan de Ayala sailed the "packet boat", *San Carlos*, into San Francisco Bay. For forty-two days he and his crew explored and mapped the bay, and its islands. The small island in the middle of the bay just inside the harbor entrance presented an interesting sight to the visiting Spaniards. It appeared to be of white rock with thousands of roosting birds. The island was actually sandstone covered with bird guano giving it the appearance of white rock. Although historians are not in total agreement as to how the island got its name, the most popular view is that Ayala named it for the large number of pelicans living there. The Spanish word for pelican was Alcatraces and the small rock outcropping came to be known as *Isla de los Alcatraces*, The Island of the Pelicans.

Until 1846 Alcatraz was generally ignored by the early California settlers. At that time Julian Workman requested permission from Pio Pico, the Mexican governor of California, to establish a navigational light on Bird Island, as it was known to many at that time. Before the plan could be carried out, however, California became a state and the island was seceded to the United States government. It soon became a military installation occupied by the United States Army Engineers, and was taken away from the many bird families living there.

Human family life came to Alcatraz in the 1850s after the 1849 discovery of gold in the foothills of the Sierra-Nevada Mountains. San Francisco soon became a bustling population center, and there was a need to protect the city and its population from foreign attack. Cannon were installed on the island as part of the city's defense, and it became known as Fort Alcatraz. The first lighthouse on the West Coast was constructed on Alcatraz to aid the large volume of ship traffic moving in and out of the harbor. With the lighthouse and fortifications came men to operate and maintain them. In addition to the fortifications and other structures that go with military life, military families came to Alcatraz.

Military family life on the island included a schoolhouse for the children, a bakery, bowling alley, library and other aspects of community living. Gardens were built where the soldiers and their families grew flowers and vegetables in small plots. Since all the soil necessary for gardens on Alcatraz had to be brought from nearby Angel Island and Marin County, agricultural activity was limited. In time the function of Alcatraz changed from a military garrison to a military prison, and the name was changed to the United States Army Disciplinary Barracks, Alcatraz. Despite the change in the island's mission, family life continued.

In 1933 the War Department decided to abandon the facility at Alcatraz because the cost of maintaining the Disciplinary Barracks was too great. The Federal Bureau of Prisons thought Alcatraz was the perfect spot for a maximum security prison, and in August of 1934 the island was converted from a Disciplinary Barracks to a Federal Prison. Family life continued on the island, only now it was the families of custodial officers and employees of the Department of Justice rather than Army families that occupied Alcatraz. By 1937, 158 adults and 64 children comprising fifty-one households as well as thirty-six bachelors occupied the island. Bird life on the island did not do well. The island residents considered the birds to be pests, and the few nests that existed were often disrupted. It was a hostile environment for the birds.

Following twenty-nine years as a federal prison, the facility was closed. The families associated with the prison moved, and once again Alcatraz became the bird sanctuary it had been throughout most of its history. Today Alcatraz is operated by the National Park Service, as part of the Golden Gate National Recreation Area. As such it serves as a sanctuary for wild life including the Western Gull.

The Western Gull Today

When Alcatraz became a National Park, all of the wild life on the island came under the stewardship of the Park Service. As a result of the Park Service's management, the population of the Western Gull increased, and today there are more than 1,000 pairs of gulls in the nesting colony. In fact Alcatraz has the third largest nesting colony of Western Gulls in Central California, and is the seventh or eighth largest colony in the world.

It is the responsibility of the National Park Service to preserve and protect the animals and other natural resources in the park for present and future generations. To accomplish this goal, Park Service personnel work diligently to protect all the birds on Alcatraz including the Western Gull. Much of the work of protecting and encouraging development of the gull colony on Alcatraz is performed by wildlife biologists working on the island virtually year-round, but particularly during the nesting season. It is their job to insure a balance between the needs of the wildlife on the island and the millions of visitors who come to enjoy Alcatraz as a national park.

During the mating season the biologists protect the nesting neighborhoods from disturbance so as many chicks as possible will hatch and develop into adult birds. This is accomplished by isolating the nests as much as possible from the visitors. Biologists tour the island daily to be sure the birds are safe and protected. They also attempt to return lost chicks to their proper nesting territory. The activities of the wildlife biologist also include rescuing sick or injured birds, and if necessary, carrying them to the Wildcare Center in nearby San Rafael where they can be treated and released back into the wild. They monitor visitor activity on the island to be sure that interference with the birds is kept to a minimum. They also insure that the birds do not create dangers for the visitors. The nesting activities of the birds are observed to prevent them from building nests too close to visitor areas, which could result in attacks by the birds on visitors near a nest.

Nests built too close to visitor areas, are dismantled so the birds will rebuild the nest in a safe location. The biologist may even take the eggs to prevent them from hatching in the hope that new eggs will be laid in a safe location. Eggs laid too close to visitor areas usually do not hatch because of the disruption caused to the normal incubation process.

The resident biologist studies and analyzes the birds' behavior, monitors the number of birds on the island and records the activities in the colony. Working alone and with citizen volunteers, the biologist collects data concerning the birds' activities that will help in the future management of the colony. This important work will make it possible for millions of future visitors to enjoy the Western Gull.

The term *gull* is derived from the medieval Cornish term *gullan* or *gwylan* and the Latin term *gula*, meaning throat and the Celtic term *wylo* meaning wail. These terms developed from one of the cries the bird makes, known as the Mew Call. During Shakespeare's time the word gull was short for gullible meaning people who would "swallow" anything, even lies. Since gulls were believed to eat everything, the name came to be applied to the bird.

There are more than forty species of gulls, and they are found in numerous habitats throughout world. Generally considered a seabird, most gulls live near the ocean, but they are also found near inland bodies of fresh and salt water such as The Great Lakes in the Northeastern United States and The Great Salt Lake in Utah. Gulls are also found at the 12,000-foot elevations in the Andes Mountains, the deserts of Chile, and even in the Arctic.

Alcatraz Wildlife Biologist Christian Hellwig with a fledgling Black Crowned Night Heron that became lost during the nesting season. The bird was taken to a nearby Wildlife Center for care.

Example of nest built in an unsafe location. The nest was on the dock, too close to the visitor's area and had to be dismantled.

Western Gulls fighting over the carcass of a dead bird.

Western Gulls fighting.

Gulls have a reputation as scavengers and are not always appreciated. The birds have humorously been described as capable of eating anything that is "not ablaze or encased in lead." Gulls, including the Western Gull, are considered by many as both bullies and pests. They swarm over possible food sources such as fishing boats, garbage dumps, and food processing plants to the annoyance of those working there. They steal food from each other as well as other species, and will invade picnic areas to snatch unattended food from picnickers. They have been described by some as the "unmitigated thugs of the bird world," while others refer to them as "survivors."

They are fierce fighters, who will attack intruders and even kill neighboring chicks that accidentally wander into a their nesting area. In his 1923 book, *The Birds of California*, naturalist William Leon Dawson said of the Western Gull: "Much that is good and all that is evil has gathered itself up into the Western Gull. [It has] an appearance of sturdiness and quality which is not easily dispelled by subsequent knowledge of the black heart within…[It] is cruel of beak and bottomless of maw…be assured that this gull asks only two questions of any living thing: First, 'Am I hungry?' (Answer, 'Yes') Second, 'Can I get away with it?' (Answer, 'I'll try.')" Another expert on the subject, the late Nobel laureate Nikolass Tinbergen, described a nesting gull colony in the following stark terms: ".a gullery (nesting colony) is no city of friends. It is indeed a city of thieves and murderers." Despite these indictments, the Western Gull is a dedicated and successful parent who maintains strong family ties.

Like most seabirds, the Western Gull is a colony dweller. Throughout the world of birds only about one species in eight lives in colonies, so the vast majority of birds live fairly solitary lives. There seem to be two basic reasons for colony living, namely feeding and protection. Colony life works well for seabirds such as the Western Gull whose food source is unpredictable yet, when located, is often abundant. They can more easily locate food sources as a group than as individual birds. In addition, the younger birds and the less adept foragers can learn feeding skills from the older, more experienced birds.

There is strength in numbers, and the birds are safer in colonies than individually. In a colony there are many birds to warn of and defend against predators. Intruders in the colony are spotted quickly and come under immediate and group attack. While the younger birds present the older birds with competition for food, the older birds tend to be the more dominant and are able to obtain the best and safest nesting sites in the middle of the colony. In general, therefore, all the gulls benefit from colony life.

The Western Gull (*Larus occidentalis*) is a large white, black, and gray bird found only along the Pacific Coast of North America. Its breeding grounds extend from British Columbia in the north to central Baja California in the south, although the birds are found even further north and south during the non-breeding season. They occupy offshore islands and rock outcroppings as well as harbor sites such as abandoned piers, islands and rocks that provide safe haven from predators. They live along a very narrow strip of coastline and are rarely seen inland. Since their primary food source is fish and marine life, they are never far from the ocean.

Between February and August, they are found in or near their numerous breeding colonies all along the coast. During the remainder of the year they forage in other coastal areas either north or south of their breeding colonies. The largest colony of Western Gulls in the world is located on the Farallon Islands, about twenty-five miles west of San Francisco Bay. This colony of more than 12,000 pairs contains approximately 50% of all the Western Gulls in California, and 30% of all such birds in the world. The world population of the Western Gull is about 40,000 nesting pairs found in less than two hundred colonies.

During the nesting season, adult birds return to their colony where breeding and chick raising takes place. Throughout the non-breeding season most birds live away from the colony, although some of them remain in the colony area the entire year. A few spend the non-breeding portion of the year long distances from the colony, but most of the birds stay fairly close to the nesting grounds. Adult gulls generally return annually to the same non-breeding location, referred to by some experts on the species as their "vacation spot."

Over the years, the Western Gull has learned to live comfortably in close proximity to humans. This is particularly true on Alcatraz where approximately a million and a half visitors a year tour the island, its trails and walkways. Human contact is important to the birds' feeding habits, for when natural food sources are inadequate the Western Gull will sustain itself on human leftovers, more commonly known as garbage.

There are two recognized sub-species of the Western Gull based on the geographical location of their nesting colonies. The more common, *Larus occidentalis occidentalis*, dwell in the area from Central California north, including Alcatraz. *Larus occidentalis wymani* inhabit the breeding and foraging grounds from Central California south to Baja California. The two varieties look very much alike, but the northern bird is larger with darker eyes and paler upper parts than the southern species. The southern bird has an all white head, while its northern counterpart will often have fine streaks of gray in its head plumage.

Western Gulls do not develop their final plumage coloring until they are approximately three years old. The adult has a white head, neck, body and tail. The wings, shoulder feathers and the back of the bird, known as the mantel, are gray. The wing-tips are black and the legs are pink. The bill is yellow with a red spot on the lower end of the beak. The coloring of the adult male and female is the same, but the males are somewhat larger than the females. Adult males usually weigh about two and a half pounds, while the females generally weigh less than two pounds. The male has a larger, heavier bill since he fights a great deal more than the female.

The feathers of the Western Gull like the feathers of all birds are one of nature's marvels, and the birds' lives depend on their feathers. A single feather is held together by as many as a million or more tiny hair-like structures that make it a flat, light-weight, flexible device with amazing qualities. Growing out of the skin of the bird like hair, the layers of feathers insulate the bird. The feathers also provide a shield against water, dust, bacteria, and other adverse elements with which the bird comes in contact. Because of their elaborate interwoven construction the feathers can withstand the rushing air over the surface of the bird during flight while still providing protection and warmth.

On occasion the feathers can become ruffled because of some exterior force during flight or in combat. When this happens sensory receptors in the skin are activated telling the bird that some of its feathers have become disrupted. The bird can then focus on the affected area and by "preening" correct the problem with its bill. Because of the way the feathers are constructed, the bird can easily correct the disruption with its bill.

Preening is done regularly by the Western Gull and it consumes about 10% of the bird's time. Preening is the smoothing, cleaning, rearrangement, and oiling of feathers with the bill, and is an important part of each bird's personal care and grooming. A preening gland at the base of the tail supplies the oil necessary to treat the feathers. The bird picks up the oil on its bill and spreads it over the rest of its body feathers. The gull rubs its head on the gland and spreads the oil over its head with its feet, since it cannot groom its head with its bill. Bathing is another form of grooming, also done regularly by the Western Gull. This involves submerging and ruffling its feathers in the water, then shaking off the excess water.

Because the bird's life depends on its feathers, it is important that they always be in a sound and healthy condition. Over time, feathers can become damaged or simply wear out to the point that they do not properly protect the bird. Since feathers, once formed, are dead material like human fingernails, they cannot be repaired. Feathers, therefore, need to be replaced. The process of replacing worn feathers is known as molting.

As feathers become worn, new ones grow and eventually force out the worn feathers. It is a process similar to the replacement of children's baby teeth with permanent teeth, and goes on throughout the life of the bird. The Western Gull goes through various molts while it is a juvenile attaining its adult plumage over a three-year period. An adult Western Gull has two molting periods a year, losing feathers from various parts of its body each summer and feathers from its head and neck in the spring. It is described as a complete molt in the summer and partial molt in the spring.

Since the price that a bird pays for flight is the loss of its arms, its bill (beak) must perform many of the functions of arms. The bill, therefore, is used for grasping, carrying, scratching, fighting, and digging. It is also a major tool for eating. Not only does the Western Gull eat with its bill, but uses it to catch, carry, and cut up its food, kill its prey, pry open shells to eat the meat inside, and move rocks, kelp, wood, and other items to find food. It builds its nests, moves its eggs, and grooms itself with its bill. The bill consists of an upper and lower jaw each wrapped in a tough layer of skin. This outer horny layer is thickest at the tip, which gets the most use and suffers the most wear.

The Western Gull is an extremely well equipped bird. It can fly, swim, walk, and run in all conditions of terrain and weather with enormous effectiveness. It propels itself swiftly along the surface of the water using its large webbed feet as underwater paddles. It is a superb flyer, able to soar effortlessly in the winds and updrafts while fishing, protecting its chicks, or challenging the aggressive conduct of its neighbors. Gulls have excellent vision, and are able to distinguish colors. As a result they can spot a possible food source from great distances. On the other hand, they have a very poor sense of smell so they have no problem feeding in smelly garbage dumps. They are robust birds with a normal life expectancy of 10-15 years, although some members of the species live as long as thirty, or forty years.

The Western Gull is dedicated to family life. They are monogamous and normally mate for life. An established pair returns to the same location in the colony each year to lay eggs and raise their chicks. The male and female birds share the responsibilities of raising their chicks similar to the human family life that existed on Alcatraz. Occasionally the offspring even return to visit their parents after they have learned to fly and are able to care for themselves.

Although frequently fighting with other birds and working hard as a dedicated parent, there is a light-hearted side to the Western Gull. When time permits the bird knows how to

Adult male Western Gull, part of the Alcatraz Colony.

Pair of adult Western Gulls during early part of nesting season.
Note the larger, male bird on the right.

Western Gull preening itself.

Adult bird bathing in the bay.

Adult bird soaring above Alcatraz.

Parents feeding chicks approximately two or three days old.

have a good time and often does. Being a highly skilled flyer, the Western Gull uses this talent for recreational purposes. The winds and updrafts around Alcatraz permit the bird to soar, dive, and glide in a playful fashion. They sail through the air engaging in what appear to be acrobatic tricks and seem to be playfully chasing one another.

They also play games with one another in flight. After feeding and having their appetites satisfied, one of the birds will catch a fish in its bill and fly by the others inviting a game of chase. The other birds will chase the bird with the fish until one of them is able to snatch the fish away. The group then chases the new possessor of the fish until the fish is again captured. The game goes on until the birds grow tired, at which time the fish is dropped, uneaten, back into the water.

Communication Among Western Gulls

Gulls communicate with one another through a series of sounds and body movements not unlike the way human families communicate. There are sounds and body movements directed to members of the family, and to birds outside the family, some of which are friendly and some that are hostile. While the Western Gull, like most seabirds, does not have a distinctive song or warble, it does have many different sounds that it makes depending on the situation. Sounds coupled with body movements carry particular meanings, and constitute a gull language.

Before they even hatch, the chicks begin to peep from inside the egg. This is the beginning of their Begging Call, (also known as Solicitation Call) which they will later use to ask their parents for food. The parents answer the chick's call from inside the egg with the Mew Call, a long single note which comforts the chick. The Mew Call has other uses as well. It is sounded in parent-offspring interactions and between adults during mating. It is exchanged between mates when they change positions on the nest during the incubation period, and is sounded during territorial disputes between neighboring birds.

The Alarm Call is a shrill cry that the birds make when a predator is observed, or in the case of the Alcatraz gulls when visitors approach uncomfortably close, but do not pose an immediate threat. If the predator or observer comes hazardously close the birds will give a Long-Call Note indicating greater danger, agitation, and the possible need to flee or fight. This may be followed by the Charge Call, which is sounded when the bird becomes airborne or is diving at the predator. When dogs are occasionally brought to Alcatraz, their presence immediately prompts such warning flights from the gulls. Dogs are a natural gull enemy and their mere presence brings an immediate, squawking swarm of gulls above the intruder.

The Long Call, also known as Trumpeting, is the most elaborate and variable of the gulls' calls. It is a series of notes, and is an individualized identification of a specific bird. It is used when one member of a pair returns from an absence. The returning bird sounds the call and the mate returns it. The variation of the Long Call that is sounded if a predator is approaching is often heard on Alcatraz during the nesting season. At that time approximately two thousand birds are present, and there are frequent occasions when agitation develops within the colony. In many cases the Alarm call is also sounded.

Within the colony, gulls develop "Alarm Call reliability." Nervous birds will frequently sound the call in the absence of real danger, and soon the other birds learn to ignore them. Birds that are considered reliable, however, are heeded when they sound the Alarm Call.

There is also a Flight Call that birds use to identify themselves when they are in flight. This call may also differ among individual birds.

The Mew Call is delivered with the bird's neck stretched forward and arched. This distinctive posture and sound is given in four situations. (1) It is sounded during courtship when the male is bringing food to his mate. (2) It is used when the birds are relieving one another from sitting on the eggs in the nest. The bird approaching the nest gives the Mew Call indicating a desire to relieve the nest sitter. If the bird on the nest wishes to be relieved it will exchange places with its mate. (3) The call is also given by the parents to call the chicks to be fed when a parent returns to the nest area with food. (4) Finally, the call is exchanged between neighboring birds signaling a territorial dispute. In that situation the sound demonstrates hostility and can indicate an intention to attack.

The Begging or Solicitation Call accompanied by a nodding or tossing of her head up and down is given by the female during mating in response to the feeding call (Mew Call) of the male. The male makes the Mew Call, the female responds with the Solicitation Call, and the male gives food to the female. If she eats the food, they mate, and later she lays the eggs.

In addition to the various sounds they make, Western Gulls also communicate through physical postures and movements. One such position is the Upright Posture and involves the bird stretching its head and neck forward. This is a threatening gesture directed at intruders. Besides stretching its neck, the bird lifts its wings slightly making it appear larger than it really is. This also prepares the bird to use its wings to strike an opponent if that becomes necessary. At the same time the bird makes the Long Call in a hostile and menacing fashion. Often this Upright Posture precedes a charge and attack on an intruder. This combination of sound and physical movement is normally engaged in by the male bird, who is the member of the pair that does most of the fighting.

The Oblique Position involves the bird holding its head erect and making the Long Call. This is the method of greeting a returning mate and is also used as a friendly greeting to neighboring birds when they return to the territory.

The Western Gull resolves territorial disputes with neighbors through a process known as Grass Pulling. In order to demonstrate ownership of a particular territory, a bird will grasp grass or other growing vegetation in its bill, stand with its feet braced wide apart, and pull vigorously in a threatening manner. This is done while facing an opponent and is usually a means of establishing a bird's territory for purposes of nesting. In the absence of vegetation, the birds may pick up sticks or pull on a nearby fence. The bird will also crouch and depress its head to make its throat appear larger and more threatening to an opponent. Territorial disputes are normally carried out by the males and the female is rarely involved in Grass Pulling

Choking is another form of communication by physical activity, and is usually performed by a mated pair together. The birds squat or crouch with their breast low to the ground and their tail elevated. The birds puff out their throat giving it a swollen look, and make a deep *huoh-huoh-huoh* sound while performing a rhythmic jerking movement of the head. (Head Tossing)This display occurs in three situations: 1) hostile territorial encounters with neighbors across a shared border, 2) between a mating pair during nest building and the early stages of courtship, and 3) during nest exchanges. Choking seems to be an indication by the communicating bird of a desire to occupy a specific physical location.

By turning and facing away from another bird, the gull indicates appeasement or lack of hostility. It is a friendly and non-threatening act.

Western Gull in the "Upright Posture."

Western Gull in the "Oblique Posture."

Western Gull in the "Head Tossing Posture."

Western Gull in the "Grass-pulling Posture."

Western Gull in the "Choking Posture."

The Parade Ground at the southern portion of the island is the scene of all forms of communication among the gulls.

Feeding Habits of the Western Gull

The feeding habits of the Western Gull vary depending upon natural conditions, the area where the birds live, and the nearness of human settlements. Gulls living in remote areas tend to limit their diet to natural forms of food, such as fish and marine life, while birds that live near human settlements will supplement their natural diet with human refuse. Such garbage is found on beaches, in parks, harbors, picnic areas, fish and chicken processing plants, fishing grounds, refuse dumps, and even city streets. Feeding habits can also be altered by changes in ocean temperatures such as the warming trends that occur during El Niño conditions in the Pacific Ocean. Oil spills, pesticides, and similar conditions can also affect the natural food supply. Like all Western Gulls, those on Alcatraz are adversely affected by the El Niño conditions.

Along the western coast of North America the California Current flows from north to south. It is part of a huge clockwise flow of water in the Northern Pacific. The prevailing wind pattern along the California coast is such that it moves the surface water of the California Current to the west and away from the coast. This causes the cooler, subsurface water near the coast to rise and become part of the surface current, a process known as Upwelling. The cool water is rich in nutrients favorable to the growth of small fish and marine life, which in turn are eaten by seabirds including the gulls. This Upwelling condition goes on from March to August, but is greatest during the spring months of April through June. It is during this period that the gulls are nesting and require the most nutritious food of the year. It is nature's natural food chain and normally it works very well.

During an El Niño winter, however, weather patterns over the Pacific Ocean change and the trade winds diminish. The decrease in trade winds reverses the normal Upwelling process, and the temperature of the surface water along the coast rises. Without the nutrients associated with the deeper, colder water the small marine life does not flourish, and there are fewer fish and other marine creatures available for the Western Gull and other seabirds to eat.

It is during periods such as El Niño that the adaptability of the Western Gull becomes important. Deprived of its normal marine diet, the Western Gull turns to human refuse as a source of food. Although not as nutritious as fish, such a diet can sustain the gulls while other species totally dependent on marine life for food may not all survive. Although most gulls prefer a fish diet, during difficult feeding periods they will not turn down left over fragments of someone's ham sandwich if that is all that is available for the bird or its family to eat. It is also during difficult feeding times that gulls increase their tendency to steal food from one another and other species.

In addition to fish, the diet of the Western Gull includes other marine creatures such as squid, sea urchins, clams, snails, muscles, red crab and others. Sometimes they will eat the eggs and chicks of other sea birds, and occasionally even small adult birds. Gulls tend to develop individual food tastes, some actually preferring to feed on garbage rather than fish. On Alcatraz some of the gulls regularly feed on leftovers in the areas set aside for picnicing. They also have a strong digestive system, and are able to regurgitate such indigestables as bones, stones, bits of plastic, etc. If necessary, the Western Gull will eat virtually anything it can find.

The gulls on Alcatraz eat a variety of fish. Anchovy and midshipmen fish are fed to the chicks, and the males feed jack-smelt, white croaker, and spotted cusk eel to the females during the pre-egg-laying period. Midshipmen fish are so named because they have glowing spots that resemble a row of buttons similar to a naval uniform. They are also known as California Singing Fish and Canary Bird Fish because of the humming sound that the male fish makes. During mating the male fish hide in small openings in and under the rocks, and their humming sound attracts the female. She enters the cave, lays her eggs, and swims away. Thereafter the male fertilizes the eggs, and remains in the cave seeking to attract another female. A collection of several males in the same area makes a sound like a huge hive of bees, and it is the female fish's job to decide in which cave she will lay her eggs.

Some male midshipmen fish are born "vocally challenged" and unable to attract females. These non-singing fish linger outside the caves. After a female lays her eggs, a non-singing male will attempt to sneak into the cave and fertilize the eggs before the occupant of the cave has a chance to do so. It is nature's way of making certain that the eggs get fertilized and new fish are born. Male midshipmen, therefore, go though life as either a singer or a sneaker.

The jack-smelt is a delicate, elongated, silvery fish also known as the silver side or the blue smelt. They can grow as large as thirteen to fifteen inches in length, live to be eight or nine years old and when fully grown can weigh as much as a pound. It is the newly hatched and very young jack-smelt that is part of Western Gull's diet.

White croaker, is also known as king-fish. They live not only in the coastal waters, but also in inland areas such as San Francisco and Bodega Bays. The Northern Anchovy have been increasing in number since the 1950s. A single female may lay up to 25,000 eggs each year. The eggs float on the surface of the water and produce a tiny larva, which grow into adult form in about three months. They grow to about four inches within the first year.

The feeding grounds of the Alcatraz Western Gull include the open areas of the bay and ocean as well as rocky shores and sandy beaches. In the open ocean the birds gather in large flocks and follow fishing boats to scavenge fish and bait that fall overboard. They also collect above schools of feeding sea lions and large fish, as well as flocks of foraging diving birds such as pelicans and cormorants. Deep water fish will often come to the surface to escape these diving birds and seals, only to be caught by the gulls on the surface. Gulls will also sit on the water or hover above schools of small fish that they can capture by dipping their bills into the water. Since the gull cannot dive very deep, it fishes from the surface. On sand and rocky beaches they locate food in tide-pools, among the rocks, in kelp beds and in the shallow waters. Here they find shellfish, which they will carry to a predetermined height from which the catch is dropped on a rock or other hard surface. This causes the shell to break, after which the bird will remove the meat from the broken shell. Not renowned for their brainpower, some young gulls have been observed dropping the same shell repeatedly into shallow water before realizing the surface was not hard enough to break the shell. Gulls have even been observed dropping tennis balls and bolts thinking they can be broken open to produce food.

Although gulls are thought of as scavengers, garbage is a relatively small part of their diet. While the Alcatraz gulls will eat scraps from picnic areas, rubbish dumps, beaches and other sites, their largest source of human refuse is from crab fishing areas near the island. Crab fisherman use raw chicken as bait in their crab traps, and frequently pieces come to the surface where they are scooped up by the gulls. Gulls turn to human refuse when fishing conditions are unfavorable and when they are incubating their eggs. Human leftovers are usually easy to find, although the quality of this food is not as good as their natural diet of fish and other marine life.

Fish is the most nutritious gull food. While the female is preparing to lay her eggs, her diet consists almost entirely of fish and other natural food that is brought to her at the nest area

Juvenile Western Gull, a year or two old, eating a fish caught in the bay.

Juvenile Western Gull approximately two years old eating raw chicken on Jefferson Street in San Francisco near Fisherman's Wharf probably purloined from a garbage can.

Juvenile Western Gulls eating from carcass of a dead juvenile in Aquatic Park, San Francisco.

Parent feeding chicks less than a week old.

Parent feeding chicks, approximately 2 to 3 weeks old.

Parent feeding nearly fledged chicks.

Fledgling begging for food from its mother.

Adult gull. Note red spot on lower part of beak believed to be used by very young chicks to focus on during feeding.

by her mate. This natural diet produces the largest and heaviest eggs as well as the strongest and healthiest chicks. The female requires a great deal of protein during the time she is forming her eggs, and fish is a good source of protein. After the eggs are laid, the adult birds are not as careful about their diets. Since they have to spend most of their time protecting and hatching the eggs, there is less time to spend fishing. As a result, they may eat more refuse since it is easier to find, and good nutrition is not as important to the female as when she was preparing to lay her eggs.

Once the chicks are hatched, however, the parents return to a diet of fish for the chicks and themselves. Chicks fed a nutritious diet are healthier, and usually grow well. Chicks fed refuse are often unhealthy and some do not survive. Chick rearing is a demanding time for the parents for they must not only find food for themselves but also for the growing chicks. The chicks cannot feed themselves for several weeks after hatching, and must be fed by their parents every few hours.

Feeding the chicks and the female before she lays her eggs is done the same way. The feeding bird collects the food and stores it in a section of its digestive tract known as the proventiculus or forestomach. When the feeding bird returns to the nest area it gives the Mew Call to the chicks or the mate announcing its return with food. It then brings the food up from its stomach and drops it on the ground for the chicks or the female to eat. When the chicks are very small the parent may actually put the food in the chick's beak so all the chick has to do is swallow it. While it sounds a little messy, it works well for the gulls.

Gulls will drink both fresh and salt water, but they prefer fresh. The excess salt is expelled from their body through salt glands located above their eyes.

The Western Gull Family Year

For established pairs, the family year of the Alcatraz Western Gull generally begins in the latter part of January or early February. During that time the adult birds return to the Alcatraz breeding colony from their winter quarters up and down the Pacific Coast. Some pairs have been together all year long while others lived apart during the winter months.

Gulls mature and begin to form pairs when the male is four and the female is five years old. Prior to that they live a solitary life as juveniles, and their plumage color changes as they mature. When they fledge (develop feathers and begin to fly) their coloring is a mottled, dark gray and brown, totally distinct from the appearance of an adult. Their bill is black unlike the yellow bill of the adult. Each year the juvenile plumage changes giving the bird a distinctive first, second, and third year appearance.

The original plumage is worn for only a few months after the birds fledge in the late spring, and in the late fall a partial molt (loss of feathers) takes place. These new feathers are a

Fully fledged chick, probably forty to fifty days old.

Juvenile bird in its first year of life.

Juvenile in it's second year.

Juvenile in it's third year.

Adult Western Gull.

Adult birds collecting on the Parade Ground at the start of the nesting season. Here young birds will find mates and prior nesting pairs will re-establish existing relationships.

Adult pair at the start of the mating/nesting season.

The Western Gull is comfortable in close quarters with it's human neighbors.

lighter gray- brown mixed with grayish white, and the bill becomes dusky rather than black.

A complete molt takes place when the bird is thirteen to fourteen months old, and the slaty blue mantle begins to appear. The bill becomes yellow. During this second year there is individual variation in the plumage development, but the overall coloring lightens with additional white appearing in the feathers. By the time they are three years old, most birds have full or nearly full adult coloring, characterized by a white head, neck, body, and tail, gray mantle, black wing tips, and yellow bill.

In forming pairs it is the female who takes the lead. She approaches the male tossing (nodding) her head up and down to get the male's attention. The male will accept her or chase her away, and they either become a pair or the search goes on. The paring may take place in the colony after the male has established his nest territory. The paring could take place away from the colony, in which case the male will establish his territory after he has a mate. Wherever paring occurs, it is a search by the young adult birds for their life long companion.

The male establishes the nesting territory, which may involve conflict with nearby birds who do not want a new nest in their neighborhood. Not all the birds return at once, but arrive intermittently some arriving as late as early June. Not only do they return to the colony, but established pairs go back to their former nesting territory, which is the exact location where the pair nested the previous year. Usually they build their nest in the same spot as the year before and sometimes a pair will simply rebuild the nest they had previously used.

The early nesters are typically the most successful parents. They tend to lay the largest number of eggs, their eggs are heavier, and their chicks are healthier with a greater survival rate than birds who arrive later. The pairs that nest early are often the older and more mature birds. They have mated and nested before, and are experienced at raising chicks. Birds breeding for the first time not only have to find a mate and go through the procedure of becoming a pair, but also have to find a nesting territory. Since the number of birds in the Alcatraz colony is growing, new nesting sites are getting harder to find. First time nesters, therefore, may have difficulty finding a place to build their nest, which can further delay the mating and chick raising process.

Juvenile and immature birds are not accepted in the colony during the breeding season, and only adult birds capable of mating are welcome. Juvenile birds that show up are usually driven away by the adult birds. They do not want juveniles around the chicks for fear they will harm them. The juveniles will also compete with the adults for food, and during the nesting season food is hard enough to find without the added competition of the non-nesting juveniles. Occasionally juvenile birds are able to remain in the colony, and will build nests and attempt to raise chicks. Because they have not yet matured they are unable to produce eggs, so nothing comes of their efforts. It is the young birds' way of playing house and pretending to be grown-ups. This practice nesting, however, may make the birds better parents once they mature.

While rare, there are occasions when a pair of Western Gulls separates. If the pair is unable to produce chicks or the male does not provide adequate food for the female in preparation for egg laying, the pair may part. Separation may also occur if the pair cannot synchronize their activities and the eggs are left unattended. If the male member of the pair dies or for some reason abandons the female, she must find a new mate and a new territory. If a female dies or abandons her mate, the male will remain in the same territory and wait to be approached by a new mate.

Once the male establishes the territory, the pair defends it together. The central area of the territory is the nest and the chicks, and this area is fiercely defended against all intruders. Area further from the nest is also defended against neighbors, but with less vigor. Early arriving birds initially defend large territorial areas. After their eggs have been laid and they are incubating, the pair remains close to the nest and will not defend as much territory as before. This may make it possible for later arriving birds to find nesting places. The size of the territory often changes during the breeding season, being largest during the chick rearing period and smaller when the eggs are being incubated. Since the chicks need room to exercise and play, larger amounts of territory are needed at that time.

There is an area on Alcatraz where the Rangers believe that gulls seeking mates tend to collect. This is the roof of the electrical shop located along one of the walkways, and is jokingly referred to by the Rangers as the gulls' "singles bar."

Here the unattached male and female birds seem to collect prior to going through the process of finding a mate. A good deal of pre-mating activity also takes on the Parade Ground, the large open area at the south end of the island that was the site of military drills and inspections during the Army's occupation of Alcatraz.

Once the nesting area is established, the pair proceeds with nest building. Both male and female dig depressions in the ground using their breast, wings, feet, and bill. After the depressions are completed they are filled with grass and other soft vegetation, feathers, seaweed, pieces of string, rope and similar material to form a nest. If the surface is cement or too hard in which to dig, the nest is built without a depression. The nest is shaped and cupped by the bird using its breast and feet. Birds nesting for the first time will each prepare one or two nests. The female makes the final choice and selects one of the nests in which to lay her eggs. The unused nests are ignored. As noted above, an established pair will build their nest in the same territory, often in the exact spot they had nested before. Each year thereafter the pair will build their nest in the same place.

The parents build their nests during the day, and try to select a site that will be safe for the chicks particularly when they are very young. The nest is frequently built near a large rock, wall, or similar object to protect it from predators, the wind and adverse weather. Effort is also made to build the nest on a level spot to make it easy and safe for the chicks to move about. Nest building is an ongoing activity with the nest being added to and maintained after the eggs have been laid and throughout the incubation period.

Once the gulls have built their nest and mated, there is a waiting period of about two weeks during which the eggs develop in the female. The female stays near the nest during this time, and the male brings food to her. This permits the female to rest and prepare for the ordeal of egg laying and chick rearing that lies ahead. When the female is ready to lay the eggs, she will sit on the nest until all the eggs have been laid.

The eggs are usually laid early in the morning and at two-day intervals. During egg laying the male continues to feed the female, who remains on or very close to the nest. The number of eggs laid by the female is called a clutch. The typical clutch is three eggs, although occasionally there are only two. Three eggs can equal up to one third of the female's weight, so it is important that she rest and eat well prior to laying them. The eggs vary in color but are normally light olive, buff, off-white, or greenish in color. Whatever color the eggs may be, they are speckled with black, brown or olive spots.

Incubation of the eggs begins when the first egg is laid. The second egg is laid two days after the first and the third is laid four or five days after the first. Generally, the first egg laid and the chick it yields are the largest, and the third egg and chick are the smallest. Once the eggs are laid one of the parents is sitting on the eggs almost continuously, protecting them and keeping them warm. The male and female share the responsibility of incubating the eggs, relieving one another every few hours.

The roof of the electrical shop, jestingly referred to by the
Rangers as the Singles Bar.

Adult male collecting material with which to build a nest.

Adult pair in the process of building their nest.

Nest building.

Example of well hidden nest.

Nesting bird incubating eggs.

Nesting bird, incubating eggs.

Nesting bird, incubating eggs.

Nesting bird, incubating eggs in rather precarious location, four stories above the Alcatraz dock.

Nest built at the Alcatraz dock in San Francisco. A highly unusual place for a nest to be built and for chicks to survive, yet in this case one of the chicks did survive to adulthood.

Nesting scene on the Parade Ground. Various nests visible in close proximity to one another.

Eggs that failed to hatch in various nests that were collected by the Biologist. It is a good example of the various color combinations of the eggs of the Western Gull.

When incubation begins three incubation, or brood patches, develop on the underside of each of the parents. These areas lose their feathers so the warm skin of the adult birds directly covers the eggs and keeps them warm. When sitting on the nest, the adult birds arrange the eggs so each egg is under a brood patch to receive the maximum amount of warmth. The female spends more time on the nest than the male, and she usually sits on the nest during the night. Because of this the female brood patches are larger that those of the male. The male sits on the nest when the female is absent, and occasionally relieves his mate while she remains within the nest territory. The eggs are hearty and can be left unattended for several hours without affecting their hatchability, but this is rarely done. Eggs left unprotected can be eaten by predators, and prolonged interruption of the incubation process can cause a delay in the hatching of the eggs.

Sometimes a clutch of eggs is lost before they hatch either because of adverse weather conditions or predators. If this happens the female requires another seven to ten days to produce a new clutch. The new eggs are usually smaller and fewer in number than the original clutch. It is not often that a second clutch is laid after the loss of the first. Only about one clutch in ten that is lost is replaced. Usually the loss of the entire clutch simply means that pair will not produce any chicks that year.

If three eggs are laid, both the first and second eggs will hatch thirty days after the first one was laid. This is the case even though the chick in the second egg is two days younger than the first. The third egg hatches either thirty-one or thirty-two days after the original egg was laid.

During the incubation period the parents communicate with one another through sounds and body movements to determine when one bird will relieve the other from sitting on the eggs. The parents take turns leaving the nest area to feed in the surrounding feeding grounds during incubation. If feeding conditions are good, the female spends more time on the nest than the male. Except when he is feeding, the male stays near the nest to protect the nest and his mate. It takes the full time activity of both parents to hatch and raise the chicks. It is dangerous for the eggs or the newly hatched chicks to be left unguarded, so at least one of the parents is always present. During the incubation period the parents are not particularly careful about their diet. If food is plentiful they will eat fish. If not, they will eat anything they can find.

Five or six days before hatching, a fine network of cracks develops on one end of the egg, and two or three days later the chick makes a hole in the cracked area. The tip of the chick's beak projects through this hole. When this occurs, the chick begins to make peeping sounds from inside the egg, and the adults respond with Mew Calls to comfort the chick. As soon as the chick makes its first sound from within the egg, the parents return to an all fish diet.

Two or three days after the hole appears in the egg, the chick is hatched. The chicks hatch in the morning. The first and second eggs hatch within a three to four hour period of one another, and the third chick hatches a day or two later. When a chick is ready to hatch it will push through the shell on its own using its feet with no help from its parents. The parents are present during the hatching process watching over the chick, and Mew Calling to comfort it, but the chick breaks out of the egg by itself. The parents are there to care for the chicks the moment they are hatched. Sometimes the eggshell remains in the nest and is crushed to become part of the nest lining. Other parents will remove the shells from the nest and discard them. If for some reason one of the eggs does not hatch, it usually remains in the nest.

The young birds are covered by a thick gray down with black spots over their entire body. They have no feathers and look nothing like the adult gulls. Their eyes are open from birth and they are able to walk immediately. They remain in the nest for several hours drying, and within a couple of days move freely about the nest territory. The parents begin feeding the chicks within hours of their hatching. Although the chicks move about in the nest area, during the first week or so they spend much of the time sleeping in the nest.

Initially their wings are just little stumps, but they extend them and begin exercising them almost immediately after being hatched. After about twenty days they begin flapping their wings, and within thirty to forty days they are practicing flight by jumping up and down while flapping their wings. They first become airborne in forty to forty-five days, and within forty five to fifty days the young Western Gull can fly satisfactorily.

During the first two or three months of their lives the chicks are totally dependent on their parents for food. Receiving their first food within hours after they are hatched, the chicks are fed every two to four hours by one of their parents. The male feeds the chicks every two to three hours and the female offers them food every three to four hours. It is believed that the red spot on the adult gull's bill helps the chick focus on the parent's bill during the early days of feeding when the parents put the food directly into the open mouth of the chick. The newly hatched chick stands with its mouth open as close as possible to the bill of the parent to get food. After a few days the parent drops the food on the ground in front of the chicks and they must compete with one another for it. The young chicks are fed small items of food that they can swallow whole. As they grow older, they are able to eat larger pieces of food, but if the items of food are too large for a chick to consume, it may have trouble surviving. The male parent spends the most time foraging and fishing, and is the principal source of food for the chicks.

Once the chicks have hatched, the parents leave the nesting territory only to obtain food for themselves and the hatchlings. After a successful fishing trip, the parent returns to the nest area, calls the chicks, and regurgitates the food for the chicks to eat. The parents do not become involved in the chicks' feeding scramble, but let the chicks fight for the food that is brought to them. Often the largest and strongest chicks are the ones who obtain the most food. That makes them even larger and stronger, which can lead to the smaller chicks not getting enough to eat. While the adult birds are caring and protective of the chicks, it is up to each chick to compete with its siblings for the food that is made available, and the parents do not intervene. This is probably part of the chicks' training to prepare them for competing for food in later life. As an adult bird, the gull must be an aggressive hunter and provider, and their education for this phase of their life starts as soon as they are hatched. In crowded nesting conditions such as some of the areas on Alcatraz the parents must be careful in feeding their chicks and guard against the possible theft of the food by a marauding nearby adult gull.

If a chick does not get enough food it may die or it may abandon its family and move to a neighboring gull family. If this happens in the first week or two of the chick's life it may be adopted by another family. After that, the adult birds begin to recognize their own chicks and will reject an outside chick as a stranger. Worse than that, they may attack the wandering chick, injuring or killing it. It is always best for the chick to stay in its own family and fight with its brothers and sisters for the food. More often than not, a chick who wanders off does not survive. 30-40% of such chicks are adopted, but 60-70% of them are attacked and do not survive.

In the nesting area the chicks run and play as brothers and sisters in human families might. While the chicks run around and play, most of their early life is spend eating and sleeping. The parents are extremely protective of the chicks, covering them with their wings to keep them warm (brooding) when they are very young and feeding them frequently with the most nutritious diet they are able to find. They will also challenge and attack any bird, animal or human that comes close to the chicks.

From the beginning the chicks have strong instincts regarding their own safety. Soon after hatching they can leave the nest, but have a keen sense of danger. They are immediately aware of an intruder, and are instinctively expert at finding places of safety. Their parents also teach them how to hide and will call the chicks to hide under the adults' extended wings. Chicks will run to a parent or hide in vegetation near the nest at the first sign of an intruder. The parents will also warn the chicks when an intruder is near. If a chick gets too far from the nest the parent will not hesitate to chase a chick and use bruising force to get it back to the nest, making it clear to the youngster that such wandering is unacceptable.

During the fledging period, the chicks continue to grow and gain strength until they are capable of flight. The chicks grow rapidly, with flight feathers appearing in fifteen to twenty days. All the feathers are fully formed within forty to fifty days. Chicks are said to have fledged when they have grown their full feather plumage necessary for flight. Flight is an instinctively learned skill, and is not taught to the chicks by their parents. As their wings grow and strengthen, the young birds flap their wings, jump up and down trying to fly, and eventually are able to fly short distances. Once they master short flights, they con-

Newly hatched chicks in the nest, 2-3 days old.

Same nest as above. Here parent is brooding the chicks, keeping them warm under her wings in the nest, while mate looks on.

Chicks in nest area approximately ten days old. Note un-hatched egg in nest in center of picture.

Closer view of chicks shown above.

Chicks shown on page 61 at 20 days.

Chicks at four weeks.

Chick at five weeks.

Chick at six-weeks, nearly fully-fledged.

Chicks at approximately six-weeks, nearly fully-fledged.

Chicks hiding instinctively in the underbrush near their nest.

Chicks hiding in the underbrush near their nest.

Photo above, those on page 66 and top photo on page 67 are views of fledgling gulls learning to fly in their nesting areas. They flap their wings to lift themselves off the ground. They jump up and down in attempts to fly, and in time are able to fly short distances

Fledglings learning to fly.

Fledglings learning to fly.

Fledgling learning to fly.

The above photo and those on pages 68 and 69 show a fledging taking one of its first fights from the nest into the water.

Leaving the nest area.

Brief flight to the water.

About to make water landing.

Flight ends with safe water landing.

A nesting pair killing a fledgling from another nest that accidentally flew into their nest area. They probably believed the invading chick presented a threat to their chicks, when in reality the
invading chick was only lost.

An adult teaching its chick to fish in the bay near the dock at
Alcatraz.

tinue to practice until they can fly longer distances and can leave the nest area for brief periods of time.

After the chick learns to fly, it must be careful where it flies. If its flight ends in a nesting territory other than its own, the adult birds in that area might attack it. Outside chicks, like any intruder, will be attacked, and a fledgling chick can be seriously injured or killed by the larger, stronger adult birds. Since the chick is usually not yet a strong flyer, it may have difficulty escaping such an assault. It is not entirely clear why such dedicated parents as Western Gulls treat chicks other than their own so viciously, but it is probably because they see the intruding chick as a threat to their own chicks.

Even when the chicks are able to fly and can leave the nesting territory, they are still dependent upon their parents for food. Chicks are fed by their parents in the nest territory for a month or so after fledging. While the parents do not teach the chicks how to fly, they will go with them into the water and teach them how to fish. In July or August, after the chicks have learned to fly, the entire family usually leaves the nesting territory. By that time the families have completed the nesting cycle, and most of the fledged chicks in the colony are able to fend for themselves. On rare occasions, however, some chicks are cared for by their parents for up to six months after they arrive in the foraging area, which is usually some distance from Alcatraz.

The Neighborhoods of Alcatraz

Just as in a human city, the seabirds of Alcatraz reside in neighborhoods or districts on the island, known technically as sub-colonies. Over the years, twenty to twenty-five neighborhoods of Western Gulls have been identified with the most desirable areas containing the largest number of birds. Bird studies and censuses taken over the years have shown that four sub-colonies are by far the most popular Western Gull nesting areas on the island.

The largest and most popular of these neighborhoods is the Parade Ground located at the southern end of the island. Here nearly a third of all the gulls on Alcatraz maintain their nests. During the nesting season the Parade Ground is completely closed to visitors providing a safe and undisturbed environment for the birds to nest.

While the Parade Ground is an extremely popular nesting site, it is a somewhat unusual location for nesting because it is so open and exposed. Generally gulls nest in areas that are protected from the weather and predators and afford hiding places for the chicks. None of these characteristics exist on the Parade Ground. Since Alcatraz has very few predators to threaten the gulls and their chicks, the protection aspect does not seem to be a concern for the birds. Because the gulls' only enemies on the island are the few ravens living there and an occasional renegade Western Gull, they feel safe on the Parade Ground despite the openness of the location. The fact that there are numerous nests in close proximity to one another seems to provide the necessary protection in the event a predator should enter the area. There is ample room for the chicks to run about and exercise and it is easy for the parents to keep watch over the chicks. Gulls like to nest in a flat area, and the Parade Ground is the largest flat area on the island. Weather does not seem to be a problem for the birds, even though many of the nests have no protection from the wind, rain, or cold.

Although the nesting spaces and activities of the gulls on the Parade Ground may appear to be a sensory extravaganza and a bedlam of wings, areas seem to be well marked and understood by the gulls. Gull colonies such as Alcatraz are often described during the nesting season as "winged chaos" seemingly without order or organization. The birds appear to be going in all directions, while squawking at and challenging one another continuously. Yet through the apparent confusion there are colony rules and procedures, and territories are generally established and respected. Once territories are fixed the vast majority of the colony follow the rules, and family life proceeds in an orderly fashion.

The second most popular nesting site on the island is the area referred to as the Cistern Area. This is a large hill behind the old prison recreation yard at the northwest end of the island. It is a more typical gull nesting area with rocks and crevices where nests can be built that are well protected and hidden. In addition there is considerable open space for the adults and hiding places for the chicks. The hill faces the lee-

Various nests on the Parade Ground with many chicks soon ready to fledge.

Ravens, the only real enemy of the Western Gull on Alcatraz.

Cistern nesting area.

Photo showing the Parade Ground and Ruble Piles, some of the most popular nesting sites on the island.

Nesting area of the Brandt's Cormorants on the northwest side of Alcatraz.

Brandt Cormorant.

Adult and chick Snowy Egrets right side of photo and two Black Crowned Night Herons at bottom left of picture.

Snowy Egrets nesting on the northwest side of the island.

Snowy Egret chick on the northwest side of Alcatraz.

Black Crowned Night Heron.

ward side of the island (away from the wind), so it is protected from the wind, fog, and other adverse forms of weather. Additionally, visitors to the island rarely go to that area, and are not permitted on the hill itself, so the birds are totally protected.

The third most popular neighborhood is the Rubble Piles on the Parade Ground. These areas are similar to the Cistern location in that they are well protected from the weather and outside disturbance yet there is ample room among the rocks for the chicks to hide and exercise. Since the public is forbidden from entering the Parade Ground and Ruble Piles during the nesting season, there is almost total protection of the birds.

The final major nesting area is the hill area between the dock and the cell house along the walkways leading from the dock to the upper level of the island. These nesting areas are totally inaccessible to the public as they are located on steep hills yet have open areas for the adults and chicks.

More than half of the Western Gulls on Alcatraz nest in these four areas, while the rest of the nests are scattered among the other approximately twenty nesting areas around the island.

But the Western Gull is not the only seabird on Alcatraz, and is not the only bird to have a neighborhood of its own. While several species of birds nest on the island, three in particular have neighborhoods of their own. The second most common seabird on Alcatraz is the Brandt's Cormorant, named for the Russian naturalist who first identified the species. The population of the Brandt's Cormorant on Alcatraz is growing rapidly. There were virtually no Brandt's on the island as recently as

1989, but a recent census found nearly 740 nesting pairs. The entire colony of Brandt's is located on the west and northwest portions of the island.

Brandt's Cormorant is the most common cormorant species in California. The name cormorant is derived from the Latin words, *Corvus Marinus*, meaning marine crow (raven). Brandt's have black, glossy plumage with black legs and feet and a long, narrow, hooked bill. They live and roost on the rocks and cliffs on the windward side of the island. Their diet is almost exclusively fish, which they catch underwater by diving and swimming rapidly using their bill to catch fish. They build their nests of seaweed very close to one another. With the nests built so close together the colony is relatively safe from air borne predators such as gulls and ravens.

Two other occupants of the island are the Snowy Egret and the Black Crowned Night Heron. Both of these species nest in the Cypress, Eucalyptus, and other trees and shrubs on the western side of the island in close proximity to one another. The Egrets build platform-like nests in the trees of twigs and branches approximately five to eight feet above the ground. Here they lay their eggs, usually 3-4 in a clutch, and raise their young. Both parents share in the incubation and chick raising activities. Snowy Egret pairs do not recognize each other except at the nest, and even there the returning mate must perform an elaborate greeting ceremony in order to avoid being attacked by its mate as an intruder. When one of the pair returns the plumes on the bird's head are raised and the incoming bird bows to the one sitting on the nest. Satisfied by this display, the sitting bird leaves the nest and the returning bird takes over. The Egret has long legs and fishes by standing motionless in shallow water spearing fish, crabs, and other amphibians with its long beak. It will also occasionally run through the water chasing schools of minnows and shrimp.

The Black Crowned Night Heron is also a tree and shrub dweller in a small colony near the Egrets. The male Heron gathers nest material and brings it to the nesting site, where the female builds the nest. Like many other seabirds, both Heron parents incubate the eggs and share responsibilities in raising the young. As the name indicates, these are nocturnal birds, who do their hunting and fishing at dawn and dusk. Their diet is fish and other small marine life. Like the Egret, they are "still fishers", who wait in shallow water for their prey to swim near them where they spear them with their bill. Herons are waders with a heavy, chunky body, short neck, relatively short legs, and a heavy, short black bill. The adult has a black cap on the top of its head with a distinctive white plume down the back of the head.

While the Western Gull may not be looked upon as a model citizen in the bird world, it is a hearty bird and even its critics agree that it is a survivor. Given the conditions that exist today, it appears that the Western Gull will have a long and successful future on Alcatraz.

There are virtually no natural enemies to threaten the Alcatraz gulls, and park personnel tightly regulate human contact with the birds. Nesting conditions are excellent and even though the size of the colony is growing, there are still many potential nesting sites so the colony can grow even larger. Feeding conditions are generally favorable with abundant supplies of fish, other marine life, and garbage available for the gulls.

The winds that have swirled about the island for centuries will endure, and the skies above Alcatraz will continue to be dotted with soaring, gliding, and diving Western Gulls who call Alcatraz Island their home.

About the Authors

Since retiring from his practice as a civil trial lawyer, Ernest B. Lageson has written five books, most of them concerning Alcatraz. As a child he lived on Alcatraz, where his father was employed as a Correctional Officer.

Mr. Lageson received a BS degree in Business Administration from the University of California, Berkeley in 1954. He spent two years as a Commissioned Officer in the Navy, thereafter graduating from Boalt Hall School of Law, University of California, Berkeley in 1959. He began his career as a Deputy District Attorney in Contra Costa County, and in 1961 joined the San Francisco law firm of Bronson, Bronson, & McKinnon. Over the next thirty-five years he established a national reputation as a civil trial attorney and concluded his active practice as a partner in the Walnut Creek law firm of Archer, McComas & Lageson

He was a member of such prestigious trial lawyer organizations as the American College of Trial Lawyers, the American Board of Trial Advocates, and the International Association of Defense Counsel. In 1986 he served as President of the Defense Research Institute, a national trial lawyer organization with a membership of approximately 25,000. He retired in 1992, and he and his wife, Jeanne, still make their home in the San Francisco Bay Area. They have two grown children, Kristine Cardall and Ernest B. Lageson III, and five grandchildren.

Jeanne Lageson and her husband were high school and college classmates, and have been married in excess of fifty years. Ms. Lageson had a highly successfully career as an elementary school teacher before retiring to become a full-time wife and mother. She assisted her husband in his various endeavors, while she managed their home and family life. She too holds a degree from the University of California, Berkeley and keeps her creativity active by gardening, painting in oils, Japanese brush painting and reading. Her e-mail address is jeannelageson@aol.com

Mr. Lageson has authored two prior books about Alcatraz, *Battle at Alcatraz*, published in 1999, and *Alcatraz Justice*, published in 2002. The books chronicle the sensational and bloody escape attempt of 1946 and the murder trial that followed. Mr. Lageson's e-mail address is lagesoneb@aol.com.

Bibliography

Ainley, David G. & Robert J. Bockelheide. *Seabirds of the Farallon Islands* 1990. Stanford University Press

Ainley, David G. & T. James Lewis, 1974. *The History of Farallon Island Marine Bird Populations* 1854-1972. The Condor 76:432-446

Bent, Arthur Cleveland, 1963. *Life Histories of North American Gulls and Terns.* United States National Museum Bulletin 113, 1963

Boarman, William J. *The Breeding Birds of Alcatraz Island: Life on the Rock.* Western Birds Vol. 20, No. 2, 1998

Carney, Karen M., Brown, Marcey E., Sydeman, William J. *The Impact of Nighttime Visitation on the Breeding Colonial Waterbirds of Alcatraz Island: Preliminary Results.* Golden Gate National Recreation Area Report November 27, 1997

Ehrlich, Paul R., Dobkin, David S., and Wheye, Darryl. *The Birder's Handbook, A Field Guide to the Natural History of North American Birds.* Simon & Schuster Inc. 1988

Fisher, James, and Lockley, R.M. *Sea Birds, An Introduction to the Natural History of the Seabirds of North America.* The Riverside Press, Cambridge, MA 1954

Golden Gate National Recreation Area Report January 27, 1998. *Baseline Monitoring and Assessment of Effects of Disturbance to Seabird Populations on Alcatraz Island, CA*

Golden Gate National Recreation Area Report March 10, 1998. *Population Monitoring for the Western Gull on Alcatraz Island, CA, 1997 Breeding Season*

Golden Gate National Recreation Area Report February 1, 1999. *Population Monitoring for the Western Gull on Alcatraz Island, CA, 1998 Breeding Season*

Golden Gate National Recreation Area Report. *Population Studies of Seabirds on Alcatraz Island, 2001*

Golden Gate National Recreation Area Report. *Population Studies of Seabirds on Alcatraz Island, 2002*

Golden Gate National Recreation Area Report. *Population Studies of Seabirds on Alcatraz Island, 2003*

Jackson, Donald Dale, *The Bad and the Beautiful: Gulls Remind Us of Us.* Smithsonian, October 1989

Pierotti, Raymond J., *Patterns of Aggression in Gulls: Asymmetries and Tactics in Different Social Categories.* The Condor 96:590-599 The Cooper Ornithological Society 1994

Pierotti, Raymond J., *Male and Female Parental Roles in the Western Gull Under Different Environmental Conditions.* The Auk 98: 532-549 July 1981

Pierotti, Raymond J. and Annett, Cynthia A., *The Birds of North America No. 174,* 1995

Spear, Larry B., Ainley, David G., and Henderson, R. Philip. *Post-Fledging Parental Care in the Western Gull.* The Condor 88:194-199, The Cooper Ornithological Society 1986